PENNY the Firedog

Chris Cochand

Tellwell Talent
www.tellwell.ca

ISBN
978-0-2288-1655-3 (Paperback)

Jason took his dog Penny everywhere he went.

When Jason went for a hike, Penny hiked too.

When Jason went to the grocery store, Penny shopped too.

When Jason was sick, Penny looked after him.

And when Jason had a party, Penny celebrated with him.

Jason was a fireman. Every time Jason went to the fire station, Penny went to the fire station too.

But when Jason went out in the fire truck, Penny had to stay behind.

"You stay here, Penny," Jason would say. "You're too small and you could get hurt."

This made Penny very sad. The fire station was a lonely place when all the trucks were gone. This made Penny want to be a fire dog even more!

There was another dog named Samson. He was big and strong. He lived at the fire station and helped the firemen with all the important jobs. He also got to ride in the trucks with them when they went out on a call. This was just not fair!

One day at the fire station, when nobody was looking, Penny snuck into one of the fire trucks and hid behind the hoses.

"This way, I'll get to go with Jason and be a real fire dog!"

Sure enough, after a little while, all the bells and lights in the station started to go off, and the firemen came running to their trucks.

No one saw Penny hiding behind the hoses – not even Jason or Samson.

The fire truck raced across town with its lights flashing and siren blaring. Penny was very excited. The truck stopped in front of a house on fire. All the firemen jumped out and started working.

Samson was helping too.

The firemen hooked their hoses to a hydrant. Samson was helping too.

With a big blast of water, the firemen started to put out the fire. Samson was helping too.

Penny watched from the fire truck. "A little dog like me can't do what Samson is doing," she thought to herself. "I'll never be a real fire dog."

Just then, she saw Jason bring a blanket from the truck and wrap it around an old woman sitting on the side of the road. Jason spoke to her for a little while before going back to help put out the fire.

Penny saw the woman sitting all alone and she looked very sad. Penny felt sad for the woman and wanted to make her feel better. She jumped out of the fire truck and sat beside the woman.

Penny nuzzled her head in the woman's lap while the firemen and Samson continued to fight the fire. The woman felt happy to have Penny with her.

When the fire was all out, Jason came back to check on the woman. To his surprise, he saw Penny there too.

"Penny!" Jason said. "What are you doing here?"

Penny turned and greeted Jason with a cheerful, "Bark! Bark!"

"It's a hard thing to watch my house catch on fire," the woman said. "I felt lonely and scared, but this little dog has been by my side keeping me company the whole time. This is the best fire dog ever!"

"Well now," Jason said with a big smile on his face, "if that's the case, maybe we should have Penny come with us in the fire truck more often."

Those words meant so much to Penny. Her tail wagged back and forth and she barked again for joy. But she never left the woman's side until it was time for the firemen to return to the station.

And from that day on, every time Jason went out in the fire truck... Penny came too!

The end.

Manufactured by Amazon.ca
Bolton, ON